How Hacker's Hack Facebook & any Pc?

About this Book

The book "How Hacker's Hack Facebook & any Pc?" consists of some of tricks & methods used by hacker's all around the world to hack any Facebook account & any Pc. Please don't use this book for any bad purpose(i.e) Hacking others Facebook account (or) others Pc but use it only to protect your account (or) Pc from hacker's!

The author of the book is not responsible for anything you do against law with the help of this book!

-Muzaffar Khan(Author)

Index

Introduction:

Despite the security concerns that have plagued Facebook for years, most people are sticking around and new members keep on joining. This has led Facebook to break records numbers with over <u>one billion monthly active users</u> as of October 2012—and around 600 million active daily users.

We share our lives on Facebook. We share our birthdays and our anniversaries. We share our vacation plans and locations. We share the births of our sons and the deaths of our fathers. We share our most cherished moments and our most painful thoughts. We divulge every aspect of our lives. We even clamor to see the <u>latest versions even before they're ready</u> for primetime.

But we sometimes forget who's watching.

We use Facebook as a tool to connect, but there are those people who use that connectivity for malicious purposes. We reveal what others can use against us. They know when we're not home and for how long we're gone. They know the answers to our security questions. People can practically steal our identities—and that's just with the visible information we purposely give away

through our public Facebook profile.

The scariest part is that as we get more comfortable with advances in technology, we actually become more susceptible to hacking. As if we haven't already done enough to aid hackers in their quest for our data by sharing publicly, those in the know can get into our emails and Facebook accounts to steal every other part of our lives that we intended to keep away from prying eyes.

In fact, you don't even have to be a **professional hacker** to get into someone's Facebook account.
It can be as easy as **running Firesheep on your computer** for a few minutes. In fact, Facebook actually allows people to get into someone else's Facebook account without knowing their password. All you have to do is choose three friends to send a code to. You type in the three codes, and voilà—you're into the account. It's as easy as that.

In this article I'll show you these, and a couple other ways that hackers (and even regular folks) can hack into someone's Facebook account. But don't worry, I'll also show you how to prevent it from happening to you.

To Understand how hackers hack facebook account's,you have to assume yourself as a hacker throughout this book because in order to catch a theif the police should think like a thief in order to catch him very easily likewise in order to understand hacker's, you have to think like a hacker!

Method 1: Reset the Password

The easiest way to "hack" into someone's Facebook is through resetting the password. This could be easier done by people who are friends with the person they're trying to hack.

- The first step would be to get your friend's Facebook email login. If you don't already know it, try looking on their Facebook page in the Contact Info section.

- Next, click on **Forgotten your password?** and type in the victim's email. Their account should come up. Click **This is my account**.

- It will ask if you would like to reset the password via the victim's emails. This doesn't help, so press **No longer have access to these?**

- It will now ask **How can we reach you?** Type in an email that you have that also isn't linked to any other Facebook account.

- It will now ask you a question. If you're close friends with the victim, that's great. If you don't know too much about them, make an educated guess. If you figure it out, you can change the password. Now you have to wait 24 hours to login to their account.

- If you don't figure out the question, you can click on **Recover your account with help from friends**. This allows you to choose between three and five friends.

- It will send them passwords, which you may ask them for, and then type into the next page. You can either create three to five fake Facebook accounts and add your friend (especially if they just add anyone), or you can choose three to five close friends of yours that would be willing to give you the password.

How to Protect Yourself from this method:

- Use an email address specifically for your Facebook and don't put that email address on your profile.

- When choosing a security question and answer, make it difficult. Make it so that no one can figure it out by simply going through your Facebook. No pet names, no anniversaries—not even third grade teacher's names. It's as easy as looking through a yearbook.

- Learn about recovering your account from friends. You can select the three friends you want the password sent to. That way you can protect yourself from a friend and other mutual friends ganging up on you to get into your account.

Method 2: Using Keylogger

Software Keylogger

A software keylogger is a program that can record each stroke on the keyboard that the user makes, most often without their knowledge. The software has to be downloaded manually on the victim's computer. It will automatically start capturing keystrokes as soon as the computer is turned on and remain undetected in the background. The software can be programmed to send you a summary of all the keystrokes via email.

CNET has Free Keylogger, which as the title suggests, is free. If this isn't what you're looking for, you can search for other free keyloggers or pay for one.

Hardware Keylogger

These work the same way as the software keylogger, except that a USB drive with the software needs to be connected to the victim's computer. The USB drive will save a summary of the keystrokes, so it's as simple as plugging it to your own computer and extracting the data. You can look through Keelog for prices, but it's bit higher than buying the software since you have the buy the USB drive with the program already on it.

How to Protect Yourself from this method:

- Use a firewall. Keyloggers usually send information through the internet, so a firewall will monitor your computer's online activity and sniff out anything suspicious.

- Install a password manager. Keyloggers can't steal what you don't type. Password mangers automatically fill out important forms without you having to type anything in.

- Update your software. Once a company knows of any exploits in their software, they work on an update. Stay behind and you could be susceptible.

- Change passwords. If you still don't feel protected, you can change your password bi-weekly. It may seem drastic, but it renders any information a hacker stole useless.

Method 3: Phishing

This option is much more difficult than the rest, but it is also the most common method to hack someone's account. The most popular type of phishing involves **creating a fake login page**. The page can be sent via email to your victim and will look exactly like the Facebook login page. If the victim logs in, the information will be sent to you instead of to Facebook. This process is difficult because you will need to create a web hosting account and a fake login page.

The easiest way to do this would be to **follow our guide on how to clone a website** to make an exact copy of the facebook login page. Then you'll just need to tweak the submit form to copy / store / email the login details a victim enters. If you need help with the exact steps, there are **detailed instructions available** by Alex Long here on Null Byte. Users are very careful now with logging into Facebook through other links, though, and email phishing filters are getting better every day, so that only adds to this already difficult process. But, it's still possible, especially if you **clone the entire Facebook website**.

How to Protect Yourself from this method:

- Don't click on links through email. If an email tells you to login to Facebook through a link, be wary. First check the URL (**Here's a great guide on what to look out for**). If you're still doubtful, go directly to the main website and login the way you usually do.

- Phishing isn't only done through email. It can be any link on any website / chat room / text message / etc. Even ads that pop up can be malicious. Don't click on any sketchy looking links that ask for your information.

Method 4: Stealing Cookies

Cookies allow a website to store information on a user's hard drive and later retrieve it. These cookies contain important information used to track a session that a hacker can sniff out and steal if they are on the same Wi-Fi network as the victim. They don't actually get the login passwords, but they can still access the victim's account by cloning the cookies, tricking Facebook into thinking the hacker's browser is already authenticated.

Firesheep is a Firefox add-on that sniffs web traffic on an open Wi-Fi connection. It collects the cookies and stores them in a tab on the side of the browser.

From there, the hacker can click on the saved cookies and access the victim's account, as long as the victim is still logged in. Once the victim logs out, it is impossible for the hacker to access the account.

How to Protect Yourself from this method:

- On Facebook, go to your **Account Settings** and check under **Security**. Make sure Secure Browsing is enabled. Firesheep can't sniff out cookies over encrypted connections like HTTPS, so try to steer away from HTTP.

- Full time SSL. Use Firefox add-ons such as HTTPS-Everywhere or Force-TLS.
- Log off a website when you're done. Firesheep can't stay logged in to your account if you log off.
- Use only trustworthy Wi-Fi networks. A hacker can be sitting across from you at Starbucks and looking through your email without you knowing it.
- Use a VPN. These protect against any sidejacking from the same WiFi network, no matter what website you're on as all your network traffic will be encrypted all the way to your VPN provider.

Method 5: Hack using Friend's Mobile

This is the most successful method ever found! Out of 10 friends,8 friends will became victim of this Method!

Step 1: Find the Victim's Facebook associated email (or) username (or)Mobile No.

Step 2: Click **Forgot Password link** in Facebook login.

Step 3: Enter victims email (or) username (or) Mobile No. Facebook will find your Victim's profile.

Step 4: Now you will get option like this **Text me a code to reset Password,** but don't click this option now.do it after step 5.

Step 5: Now ask your Friend his mobile by saying something like this "I need to call pls give your Mobile"

Step 6: Now click on **Text me a code to reset Password**

Step 7: Now Facebook will send a confirmation code to your friend's mobile which is in your hand via sms.

Step 8: Memorize that code & delete the sms

Step 9: Enter that code in password recovery page & change your password whatever you want.

Step 10: voila! The account is hacked!

How to Protect Yourself from this method:
- Always lock your mobile Inbox with security code!

Method 6: Using Stealers to Hack Facebook

Almost 80% percent people use stored passwords in their browser to access the facebook, This is is quite convenient but can sometimes be extremely dangerous, Stealers are software's specially designed to capture the saved passwords stored in the victims browser, Stealers once FUD can be extremely powerful. If you want to how stealers work and how you can set up your own one?, Kindly refer the link
http://www.mediafire.com/?686o7c3j1euxwm8

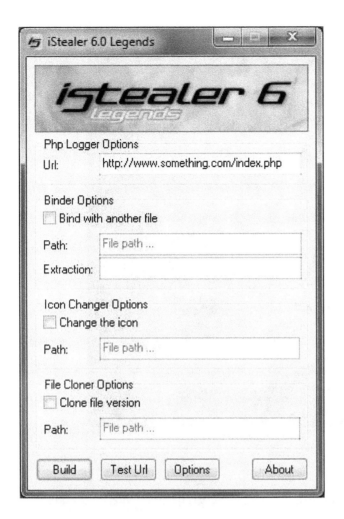

How to Protect Yourself from this method:

- Never save password's in your browser!

Method 7: Mobile Phone Hacking

Millions of Facebook users access Facebook through their mobile phones. In case the hacker can gain access to the victims mobile phone then he can probably gain access to his/her Facebook account. Their are lots of Mobile Spying softwares used to monitor a Cellphone.

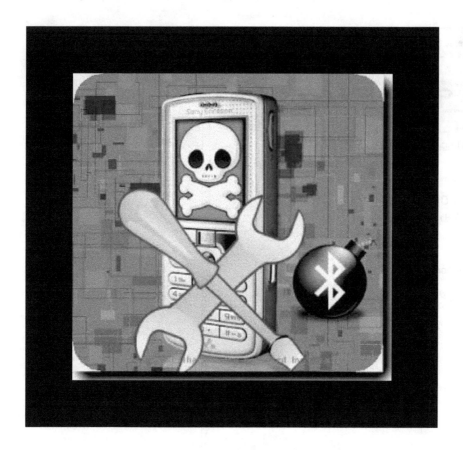

The most popular Mobile Phone Spying softwares are:

1. Mobile Spy
2. Spy Phone Gold

How to Protect Yourself from this method:
- Set security code for installing any application in your mobile phone so that the hacker can't install any spyware in it by getting your mobile!

Method 8: DNS Spoofing

If both the victim and attacker are on the same network, an attacker can use a DNS spoofing attack and change the original facebook.com page to his own fake page and hence can get access to victims facebook account.

Follow this link to see video how this method works:
https://www.youtube.com/watch?feature=player_embedded&v=LU2tS2ip1f8

How to Protect Yourself from this method:
- Always check the URL before entering your username & password whether it is www.facebook.com (or) something else!

Method 9: USB Hacking

If an attacker has physical access to your computer, he could just insert a USB programmed with a function to automatically extract saved passwords in the browser, I have also posted related to this attack which you can read by accessing the link below:

http://www.rafayhackingarticles.net/2010/05/usb-password-stealer.html

How to Protect Yourself from this method:
- Never save password's in your browser!

- Lock the USB port with password so non-authorized persons can't install any bad softwares in your PC!

Method 10: Man in the Middle Attack

If the victim and attacker are on the same lan and on a switch based network, A hacker can place himself b/w the client and the server or he could also act as a default gateway and hence capturing all the traffic in between, ARP Poisoning which is the other name for man in the middle attacks is a very broad topic and is beyond the scope of this article, We have written a couple of articles on man in the middle attacks which canb
be accessed from the links mentioned below: -

http://www.rafayhackingarticles.net/2011/03/man-in-middle-attack-sll-hacking.html

Protecting Yourself: Less Is More

Social networking websites are great ways to stay connected with old friends and meet new people. Creating an event, sending a birthday greeting and telling your parents you love them are all a couple of clicks away.

Facebook isn't something you need to steer away from, but you do need to be aware of your surroundings and make smart decisions about what you put up on your profile. The less information you give out on Facebook for everyone to see, the more difficult you make it for hackers.

If your Facebook account ever gets hacked, check out our guide on **getting your hacked Facebook account back** for information on restoring your account.

Bonus: If you're interested in who's checking you out, there are some ways you can (kindof) **track who's viewed your Facebook profile**.

Tricks & Methods used by Hacker's to hack any PC:

1.SYSTEM INTRUSION IN 15 SECONDS

System intrusion in 15 seconds, that's right it can be done. If you possess certain security flaws your system can be broken into in less that 15 seconds.

To begin this chapter I'd like you to do the following. Connect to the Internet using your dial up account if you are on dial up. If you are on dedicated service like High Speed connections (ie,
Cable and DSL) then just proceed with the steps below.

☐   Click **Start**

☐   Go to **Run**

☐   Click **Run** (It's a step by step manual) : -)

☐   Type **W inipcfg**

☐   Hit the **Enter** Key

This should bring up a window that looks like the following

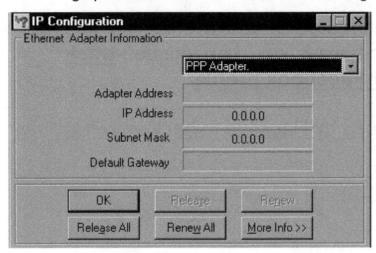

* For editorial reason the above info has been omitted *

What you should see under IP address is a number that looks something like this.

207.175.1.1 (The number will be different.)

If you use Dial Up Internet Access then you will find your IP address under PPP adapter. If you have dedicated access you will find your IP address under another adapter name like (PCI Busmaster, SMC Adapter, etc.) You can see a list by clicking on the down arrow.

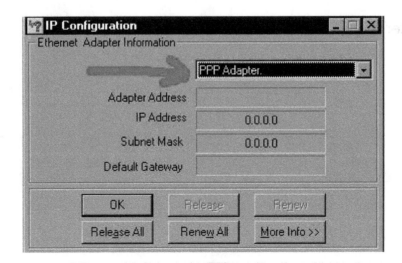

Once you have the I P address write it down, then close that window by clicking (OK) and do the following.

☐ Click **Start**

☐ Go to **Run** (Click on **Run**)

☐ Type command then Click **OK**

At this point you should see a screen that looks like this.

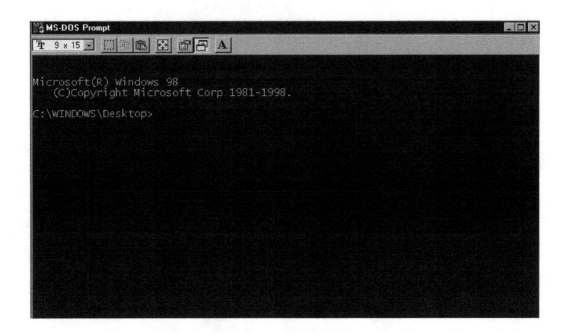

Type the following at the Dos Prompt

☐ **N btstat – A I P address**

For example: nbtstat –A 207.175.1.1

(Please note that you must type the A in capitol letters.)

This will give you a read out that looks like this

NetBIOS Remote Machine Name Table

Name	Type	Status
J-1	< 00> UNI QUE	Registered
WORK	< 00> GROUP	Registered
J-1	< 03> UNI QUE	Registered
J-1	< 20> UNI QUE	Registered
WORK	< 1E> GROUP	Registered
WORK	< 1D> UNI QUE	Registered
__MSBROWSE__.< 01> GROUP		Registered

(Again info has been omitted due to privacy reasons)

The numbers in the < > are hex code values. What we are interested in is the "Hex Code" number of < 20> . I f you do not see a hex code of < 20> in the list that's a good thing. I f you do have a hex code < 20> then you may have cause for concern. Now you're probably confused about this so I'll explain.

A hex code of < 20> means you have file and printer sharing turned on. This is how a "hacker" would check to see if you have "file and printer sharing" turned on. If he/ she becomes aware of the fact that you do have "file and printer sharing" turned on then they would proceed to attempt to gain access to your system .

(N ote: To exit out of the DOS prom pt W indow , Type Exit and hit Enter)

I'll show you now how that information can be used to gain access to your system .

A potential hacker would do a scan on a range of IP address for systems with "File and Printer Sharing" turned on. Once they have encountered a system with sharing turned on the next step would be to find out what is being shared.

This is how:

N et view \ \ < insert ip_ address here>

Our potential hacker would then get a response that looks something like this.

Shared resources at \ \ ip_address

Sharename	Type	Comment
MY DOCUMENTS	Disk	
TEMP	Disk	

The command was completed successfully.

This shows the hacker that his potential victim has their My Documents Folder shared and their Temp directory shared. For the hacker to then get access to those folders his next command will be.

Net use x: \ \ < insert IP address here> \ temp

If all goes well for the hacker, he/ she will then get a response of

(The command was completed successfully.)

At this point the hacker now has access to the TEMP directory of his victim .

> Q. The approximate time it takes for the average hacker to do this attack?

> R. 15 seconds or less.

Not a lot of time to gain access to your machine is it? How many of you had "File and Printer Sharing" turned on?

Ladies and Gentlemen: This is called a Netbios attack. If you are running a home network then the chances are you have file and printer sharing turned on. This may not be the case for all of you but I'm sure there is quite a number of you who probably do. If you are sharing resources please password protect the directories.

Any shared directory you have on your system within your network will have a hand holding the folder. Which looks like this.

You can check to find which folders are shared through Windows Explorer.

- ☐ Click On Start

- ☐ Scroll Up to Programs

At this point you will see a listing of all the different programs on your system

Find Windows Explorer and look for any folders that look like the above picture.

Once you have found those folders password protect them !

2.THE TROJAN "HORSE"

I found it necessary to devote a chapter to Trojans. Trojan's are probably the most compromising of all types of attacks. Trojans are being released by the hundreds every week, each more cleverly designed that the other. We all know the story of the Trojan horse probably the greatest strategic move ever made.

In my studies I have found that Trojans are primarily responsible for almost all Windows Based machines being compromised.

For those of you who do not know what Trojans are I 'll briefly explain. Trojans are small programs that effectively give "hackers" remote control over your entire Computer.

Some common features with Trojans are as follows:

- ☐   Open your CD- Rom drive

- ☐   Capture a screenshot of your computer

- ☐   Record your key strokes and send them to the "Hacker"

- ☐   Full Access to all your drives and files

- ☐   Ability to use your computer as a bridge to do other hacking related activities.

- ☐   Disable your keyboard

- ☐   Disable your mouse…and more!

Let's take a closer look at a couple of m ore popular Trojans:

- ☐   Netbus

- ☐   SubSeven

The Netbus Trojan has two parts to it as almost all Trojans do. There is a Client and a Server. The server is the file that would have to get installed on your system in order to have your system compromised. Here's how the hack would go.

The Hack

Objective: Getting the potential victim to install the server onto his/ her system .

Method 1

Send the server file (for explanation purposes we'll call the file netbusserver.exe) to you via E- Mail. This was how it was originally done.

The hacker would claim the file to be a game of some sort. When you then double click on the file, the result is nothing. You don't see anything. **(Very Suspicious)**

N ote: (How m any tim es have you double clicked on a file som eone has sent you and it apparently did nothing)

At this point what has happened is the server has now been installed on your system . All the "hacker" has to do is use the Netbus Client to connect to your system and everything you have on your system is now accessible to this "hack er."

With increasing awareness of the use of Trojans, "hackers" became smarter, hence method 2.

Method 2

Objective: Getting you to install the server on your system .

Let's see, how many of you receive games from friends? Games like hit gates in the face with a pie. Perhaps the game shoot Saddam? There are lots of funny little files like that. Now I 'll show you how someone intent on getting access to your computer can use that against you.

There are utility programs available that can combine the ("server" (a.k.a. Trojan)) file with a legitimate " executable file." (An executable file is any file ending in . exe) . It will then output another (.exe) file of some kind. Think of this process as mixing poison in a drink.

For Example:

Tomato Juice + Poison = something

Now the result is not really Tomato Juice anymore but you can call it whatever you want. Same procedure goes for combining the Trojan with another file.

For Example:

The "Hacker" in question would do this: (for demonstration purposes we'll use a chess game)

N am e: chess.exe (nam e of file that starts the chess gam e)

Trojan: netbusserver .exe (The Trojan)

 (Again for explanation purposes we'll call it that)

The joiner utility will combine the two files together and output 1 executable file called:

< insert nam e here> .exe

This file can then be renamed back to chess.exe. It's not exactly the same Chess Game. I t's like the Tomato Juice, it's just slightly different.

The difference in these files will be noticed in their size.

The original file: chess.exe   size: 50,000 bytes

The new file (with Trojan):   chess.exe   size: 65,000 bytes

(Note: These numbers and figures are just for explanation purposes only)

The process of joining the two files, takes about 10 seconds to get done. Now the "hacker" has a new chess file to send out with the Trojan in it.

Q. What happens when you click on the new chess.exe file?

Answer: The chess program starts like normal. No more suspicion because the file did something. The only difference is while the chess program starts the Trojan also gets installed on your system .

Now you receive an email with the attachment except in the format of chess.exe.

The unsuspecting will execute the file and see a chess game. Meanwhile in the background the "Trojan" gets silen tly installed on your computer.

If that's not scary enough, after the Trojan installs itself on your computer, it will then send a message from your computer to the hacker telling him the following information.

Usernam e: (A nam e they call you)

I P Address: (Your I P address)

Online: (Your victim is online)

So it doesn't matter if you are on dial up. The potential hacker will automatically be notified when you log on to your computer.

You're probably asking yourself "how likely is it that this has happened to me?" Well think about this. Take into consideration the second chapter of this manual. Used in conjunction with the above mentioned methods can make for a deadly combination.

These methods are just but a few ways that "hackers" can gain access to your machine.

Listed below are some other ways they can get the infected file to you.

New s Groups:

By posting articles in newsgroups with file attachments like (mypic.exe) in adult newsgroups are almost guaranteed to have someone fall victim .

Don't be fooled though, as these folks will post these files to any newsgroups.

Grapevine:

Unfortunately there is no way to control this effect. You receive the file from a friend who received it from a friend etc. etc.

Em ail:

The most widely used delivery method. I t can be sent as an attachment in an email addressed to you.

Unsafe W eb sites:

Web sites that are not "above the table" so to spe ak. Files downloaded from such places should always be accepted with high suspicion.

I RC:

On IRC servers sometimes when you join a channel you will automatically get sent a file like "mypic.exe" or " sexy.exe" or sexy.jpg.vbs something to that effect. Usually you'll find wannabe's are at fault for this.

Chat Sites:

Chat sites are probably one of the primary places that this sort of activity takes place. The sad part to that is 80% are not aware of it.

As you can see there are many different ways to deliver that file to you as a user. By informing you of these methods I hope I have made you more aware of the potential dangers around you. In Chapter 3 we'll discuss what files should be considered acceptable.

3:Unknown Files

From the last chapter you're probably asking yourself what exactly is safe to accept as a file from anyone. Hopefully I'll answer most if not all your questions about what types of files can be considered safe or more to the point normal.

I'll show you what normal extensions should be for different types of files and what type of files should never come in .exe formats.

We'll start with something I'm sure most if not all folks have had happen to them at least once.

PI CTURES

> Ever had someone send you a picture of themselves? I f you hang around on a chat site of any kind then chances are you've met someone or a group of people perhaps who've wanted to send you their picture. I f they did then hopefully it was not in the form of **(m ypic.exe)** . If it was you may want to run a virus check on those files in particular.

For all intensive purposes pictures should really only come in the formats listed below.

☐ Jpg (jpeg)   For example (steve.jpg)

☐ Bmp (bitmap) For example (steve.bmp)

☐ TI FF   (Tag   Image   File   Format)
     For example (steve.tiff)

☐ Gif   (Graphics   I nterchange   Format)
     For example (steve.gif)

These are all legitimate!

Your browser can view almost all of these files short of the tiff format. Other programs that can be used to view these files are Photoshop, Paintshop, Netscape, Internet Explorer and Imaging just to name a few.

W ARNI NG!

These are the file types by which images should come as. Anything else should be unacceptable. There is no reason to have an I mage of any kind come as a .exe file. Don't ever accept the excuse that it's an auto extracting image file!

READ ME AND TEXT FI LES

Almost all program information documents on the net come in one of these formats. These files are simply information documents typed up in some word processing program or text editor.

 Some examples of their extensions are:

☐ DOC   Document format for Microsoft Word, Word.
        Example: (readme.doc)

☐ TXT   Text format file can be opened by Notepad, Word,
        Microsoft   Word.
        Example: (readme.txt)

☐ RTF   (Rich Text Format)

For Example:

☐   < anything> .com

☐   < anything> .exe

☐   < anything> .txt.vbs

There is no reason for any files to be sent to you in any of the above formats if they are text documents. I can also assure you there is no reason a file should have a double extension. Such files if you should ever receive them should be treated with suspicion.

By no m eans should you ever open a file if you do not know w

hat type of file it is.

If you are uncertain about what a file type is here is a method by which you can check. Go to your favorite search engine for example:

Altavista: http: / / www.altavista.com

Or

Metacrawler: http: / / www.metacrawler.com

    ☐   Click into the search field

(Then type the file type you are inquiring about for example)

    ☐   Doc file type

    ☐   Exe file type

    ☐   Rtf file type

This will pull up sites that will give a more detailed explanation of exactly what type of file it is.

You can use the above information to better understand what type of files you receive from individuals. Without risking installing anything on your machine.

We've covered methods by which your computer can be accessed by a Netbios Attack, how files can be infected, and how they can be delivered. In Chapter 4 we'll discuss who is responsible for these attacks. We will look at the type of individuals behind the keyboard responsible for these attacks.

4: WHO ARE HACKERS?

I feel it is necessary to clarify the term hacker. Perhaps your definition of a hacker has been influenced and tainted over the years. There have been various computer related activities attributed to the term "hacker", but were greatly m isunderstood. Unfortunately for the people who are truly defined within the underground tech world as a "hacker" this is an insult to them .

There are various types of "hackers", each with the ir own agenda. My goal is to help protect you from the worst of them .

Anarchist Hackers

These are the individuals who you should be weary of. Their sole intent on system infiltration is to cause damage or use information to create havoc. They are primarily the individuals who are responsible for the majority of system attacks against home users. They are more likely to be interested in what lies on another person's machine for example yours.

Mostly you'll find that these individuals have slightly above computer skill level and consider themselves hackers. They glorify themselves on the accomplishments of others. Their idea of classing themselves as a hacker is that of acquire programs and utilities readily available on the net, use these programs with no real knowledge of how these applications work and if they manage to "break" into someone's system class themselves as a hacker. These individuals are called "Kiddie Hackers."

They use these programs given to them in a malicious fashion on anyone they can infect. They have no real purpose to what they are doing except the fact of saying "Yeah! I broke into < insert name here> computer!" It gives them bragging right s to their friends.

If there is any damage to occur in a system being broken into these individuals will accomplish it.
These individuals are usually high school students. They brag about their accomplishments to their friends and try to build an image of being hackers.

Hackers

A hacker by definition believes in access to free information. They are usually very intelligent people who could care very little about what you have on your system . Their thrill comes from system infiltration for information reasons. Hackers unlike "crackers and anarchist" know being able to break system security doesn't make you a hacker any more than adding 2+ 2 makes you a mathematician. Unfortunately, many journalists and writers have been fooled into using the word 'hacker." They have attributed any computer related illegal activities to the term "hacker."

Real hackers target mainly government institution. They believe important information can be found within government institutions. To them the risk is worth it. The higher the security the better the challenge. The better the challenge the better they need to be. Who's the best keyboard cowboy? So to speak!

These individuals come in a variety of age classes. They range from High School students to University Grads. They are quite adept at programming and are smart enough to stay out of the spotlight.

They don't particularly care about bragging about their accomplishments as it exposes them to suspicion. They prefer to work from behind the scenes and preserve their anonymity.

Not all hackers are loners, often you'll find they have a very tight circle of associates, but still there is a level of anonymity between them . An associate of mine once said to me "if they say they are a hacker, then they're not!"

Crackers

For definition purposes I have included this term . This is primarily the term given to individuals who are skilled at the art of bypassing software copyright protection. They are usually highly skilled in programming languages.

They are often confused with Hackers. As you can see they are similar in their agenda. They both fight security of some kind, but they are completely different "animals."

Being able to attribute your attacks to the right type of attacker is very important. By identifying your attacker to be either an Anarchist Hacker or a Hacker you get a better idea of what you're up against.

"Know your enemy and know yourself and you will alw ays be victorious..."

5:Tools used by Hackers

What is a carpenter without a hammer? "Hackers" re quire tools in order to attempt to compromise a systems security. Some tools are readily available and some are actually written by other hackers, with the sole intent of being used for system break- ins. Some "hackers' use a little ingenuity with their attacks and don't necessarily rely on any particular tool. In the end however it boils down to they need to infect your system in order to compromise it.

To better understand the means by which "hackers" compromise system security I feel it important to understand what tools they use. This will give you as a user insight as to what exactly they look for and how they obtain this information. In this section, I also explain how these tools are used in conjunction with each other.

<u>Port Scanners</u>

What is a port scanner?

A port scanner is a handy tool that scans a com puter looking for active ports. With this utility, a potential " hacker" can figure out what services are available on a targeted com puter from the responses the port scanner receives. Take a look at the list below for reference.

Starting Scan.

Target Host: www.yourcompany.com

TCP	Port	: 7	(echo)
TCP	Port	: 9	(discard)
TCP	Port	: 13	(daytim e)
TCP	Port	: 19	(chargen)
TCP	Port	: 21	(ftp)
TCP	Port	: 23	(telnet)
TCP	Port	: 25	(sm tp)
TCP	Port	: 37	(tim e)
TCP	Port	: 53	(dom ain)
TCP	Port	: 79	(finger)
TCP	Port	: 80	(www)
TCP	Port	: 110	(pop)
TCP	Port	: 111	(sunrpc)

Finished.

Scanning for open ports is done in two ways. The first is to scan a single I P address for open ports. The second is to scan a range of I P address to find open ports.

Try to think about this like calling a single phone- num ber of say 555- 4321 and asking for every extension available. I n relation to scanning, the phone- num ber is equivalent to the I P address and the extensions to open ports.

Scanning a range of I P address is like calling every num ber between 555- 0000 to 555- 9999 and asking for every extension available at every num ber.

Tr oj a ns

Trojans are definitely one of the tools that " hackers" use. There are hundreds of Trojans. To list them all would m ake this m anual extrem ely long. For definition purposes we'll focus on a couple.

Sub Seven

The Sub Seven Trojan has m any features and capabilities. I t is in m y opinion by far the m ost advance Trojan I have seen. Take a look at som e of the features of Sub Seven.

- address book
- WWP Pager Retriever
- UI N2I P
- rem ote I P scanner
- host lookup
- get Windows CD- KEY
- update victim from URL
- I CQ takeover
- FTP root folder
- retrieve dial- up passwords along with phone num bers and usernam es
- port redirect
- I RC bot . for a list of com m ands
- File Manager bookm arks
- m ake folder, delete folder [em pty or full]
- process m anager
- text 2 speech
- Restart server
- Aol I nstant Messenger Spy
- Yahoo Messenger Spy
- Microsoft Messenger Spy
- Retrieve list   of I CQ uins and passwords
- Retrieve list   of AI M users and passwords
- App Redirect
- Edit file
- Perform clicks on victim 's desktop
- Set/ Change Screen Saver settings [Scrolling Marquee]
- Restart Windows [see below]
- Ping server
- Com press/ Decom press files before and after transfers
- The Matrix
- Ultra Fast I P scanner
- I P Tool [Resolve Host nam es/ Ping I P addresses]

Continued…

☐ Get victim 's hom e info [not possible on all servers] :

- Address
- Bussiness nam e
- City
- Com pany
- Country
- Custom er type
- E- Mail
- Real nam e
- State
- City code
- Country code
- Local Phone
- Zip code

And m ore…

I think you get the picture of just exactly what that Trojan is capable of. Here is a picture of what SubSeven looks like.

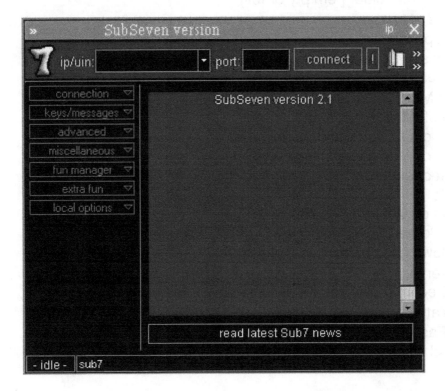

N et bus:

NetBus is an older Trojan however nonetheless is still used. I t
consists of a server and a client - part . The server-
part is the program which m ust be running on your
com puter . This should give you an idea of what Netbus is
capable of.

Netbus Features:

- Open/ close the CD- ROM once or in intervals (specified in seconds) .
- Show optional im age. I f no full path of the im age is given it will look for it in the Patch- directory. The supported im age- form ats is BMP and JPG.
- Swap m ouse buttons – the right m ouse button gets the left m ouse button's functions and vice versa.
- Start optional application.
- Play optional sound- file. I f no full path of the sound- file is given it will look for it in the Patch- directory. The supported sound- form at is WAV.
- Point the m ouse to optional coordinates. You can even navigate the m ouse on the target com puter with your own.
- Show a m essage dialog on the screen. The answer is always sent back to you.
- Shutdown the system , logoff the user etc.
- Go to an optional URL within the default web- browser .
- Send keystrokes to the active application on the target com puter . The text in the field " Message/ text" will be inserted in the application that has focus. (" | " re presents enter) .

- Listen for keystrokes and send them back to you.
- Get a screendum p (should not be used over slow connections) .
- Return inform ation about the target com puter .
- Upload any file from you to the target com puter. With this feature it will be possible to rem otely update Patch with a new version.

- I ncrease and decrease the sound- volum e.
  - Record sounds that the m icrophone catch. The sound is sent back to you.
- Make click sounds every tim e a key is pressed.
  - Download and deletion of any file from the target . You choose which file you wish to download/ delete in a view that represents the harddisks on the target .
  - Keys (letters) on the keyboard can be disabled.
  - Password- protection m anagem ent .
  - Show, kill and focus windows on the system .
  - Redirect data on a specified TCP- port to another host and port .

  - Redirect console applications I / O to a specified TCP- port (telnet the host at the specified port to interact with the application) .
  - Configure the server- exe with options like TCP- port and m ail notification.

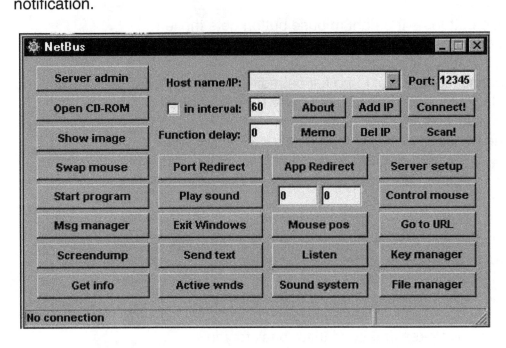

This is what the Netbus client looks like.

Joiner s

Earlier you saw me m ake references to utilities that
com bine two executable files into one. That's what these program s are. These
program s m ake it possible to hide the Trojans in legitim ate files.

I CQ

Though as itself is not a utility for hacking there are program files written by Un-
nam ed program m ers for it . The m ore advance Trojans have the ability to
notify the
" hacker" via I CQ of whether or not you are online. Given that you are infected
with a Trojan.

I f you are not infected then I CQ can serve as a Utility to give away your I P
address. Currently there are
files/ program s available on the net that allows you to
" patch" I CQ so it reveals the I P num bers of anyone on the " hackers" list . There
are also files that allow yo u add users in I CQ without their authorization or
notification.

For dem onstration purposes let's see how a hack would go if a hacker with the
above m entioned utilities were to attem pt to hack into a users m achine.

H a ck 1 :

Objective: Obtain entry to the users m achine.

Step1:   Obtain user's I CQ #
Step2:   Add User to I CQ list
Step3:   Use Get I nfo on user
Step4:   Record User's I P address
Step5:   Start a dos prom pt
Step6:   nbtstat –A < ipaddress>
Step7:   Look for hex code < 20>
Step8:   (Assum ing a hex of < 20> is there) net view
              \ \ ip_address.
Step9:   See what shares are available we'll say " C" is being
              shared.
Step10: net use x: \ \ ip_address\ c

Access to the user's m achine has been achieved.

I n the above scenario our " potential hacker" used t he patch program s available
for I CQ to gain the I P address of the

" victim " and then launch his assault .

With the realization of how an " individual" can gai n access to your m achine let's m ove on to Chapter 6. We will discuss what's at risk once your com puter has been
com promised.

FINAL WORDS

Congratulations! You've made it to the end of the manual. That's probably not an accomplishment for books of the same length. But this manual is different. You can always make reference back to this manual whenever you have questions. I t's like a manual and course in one. Learning the system loop holes and tricks that "hackers" use is only half the process. Protecting your privacy is 90% up to you, the rest can be handled by software.

You have the means and ability to protect yourself. By reading this manual alone you have proven that. You may think to yourself that you're out gunned on the Internet, don't. We all have to start learning from somewhere. Even hackers and so called "hackers" had to start learning somewhere. No one was born with the knowledge of how a computer works.

The I nternet is a tool by which many of these "hack ers" educate themselves. You can do the same. It remains the most powerful tool for information and development there is.

More and more businesses and services are migrating to the online world. You can either, sit back and watch it go, or jump on the bandwagon and ride it out. It's all up to you.

Exercise caution when dealing with people online, but don't be too paranoid. Enjoy the power of the Internet it can be a great asset to you or your business.

The online population is growing exponentially. With the recent growth of dedicated access your computer is connected to the Internet 24hrs a day. High speed access gives you the opportunity to download files at lightning fast rates. It's a long way from the old dial up BBS's. As technology increases so must your awareness.

Realistically most of us don't care about the inner workings of the Internet. Perhaps we have a sheer curiosity of what happens behind the scenes, but none of us really believes it makes a lot of difference to us to know that information. We primarily care about getting our daily activities done and enjoying the power of the Internet. We want to be able to Log online talk to our friends and family and use the Internet as tool for our benefit.

The I nternet connects you to the world where if a friends from Australia wishes to talk to you live one on one they can flip on their webcams turn on their mics and have a video conference. I t's a cut above a phone call for a fraction of the price. Don't let
"hackers" turn future advancements into unwanted ni ghtmares.

You as a user can prevent this by being careful. Take the extra necessary steps to protect yourself. When compared to the benefits you can have it definitely is worth an extra 1hr-2hrs of your time.

Don't stop learning, read all you can. Why not? You've got the world at your fingertips and information at every turn. But most importantly when all is said and done, take back your privacy from those who may seek to compromise it.

With Great Respect
Thank You!